Words of
JOY

For Barbara,
With my love
and special appreciation
for all your help this
first week of school.
September 2, 1988
Anne Green
Lumpkin County Kindergarten
Extension

Original edition published in English under the title
Words of Joy by Lion Publishing, Tring, England,
copyright © 1974 Lion Publishing.

First published in the United States and Canada in
1983 by Thomas Nelson Publishers.

Published in Nashville, Tennessee, by Thomas Nelson,
Inc. and distributed in Canada by Lawson Falle, Ltd.,
Cambridge, Ontario.

Photographs by Lion Publishing/David Alexander.

Scripture quotations are from the *Good News Bible*—Old
Testament: Copyright © American Bible Society 1976;
New Testament: Copyright © American Bible
Society 1966, 1971, 1976.

ISBN 0-8407-5336-5

Printed in Hong Kong

Words of
JOY

Thomas Nelson Publishers
Nashville • Camden • New York

SING FOR JOY

Sing to the Lord, all the world!
Worship the Lord with joy,
come before him with happy songs!

Never forget that the Lord is God.
He made us, and we belong to him;
we are his people, we are his flock.

Enter the Temple with thanksgiving;
go into its courts with praise.
Give thanks to him and praise him.

The Lord is good;
his love is eternal
and his faithfulness lasts forever.

PSALM 100

A gateway into the ancient Temple area in the old city of
Jerusalem.

YOU HAVE DONE GREAT THINGS

You answer us, . . . and you do wonderful
things to save us.
People all over the world
and across the distant seas trust in you.

You set the mountains in place by your strength,
showing your mighty power.
You calm the roar of the seas
and the noise of the waves;
you calm the uproar of the peoples.

The whole world stands in awe
of the great things that you have done.
Your deeds bring shouts of joy from one end of
the earth to the other.

PSALM 65:5–8

The sunlit waves of the Sea of Galilee, looking across to the
mountains on its western shore.

A NEW SONG

Sing a new song to the Lord!
Sing to the Lord, all the world!
Sing to the Lord, and praise him!
Proclaim every day the good news that he has
saved us!
Proclaim his glory to the nations,
his mighty acts to all peoples.

The Lord is great, and is highly praised;
he is to be honored more than all the gods.
The gods of all other nations are only idols,
but the Lord created the heavens.
Glory and majesty surround him;
power and beauty fill in his temple. . .

Be glad, earth and sky!
Roar, sea, and every creature in you;
be glad, fields, and everything in you!
The trees in the woods will shout for joy
When the Lord comes to rule the earth.
He will rule the peoples of the world
with justice and fairness.

PSALM 96:1–6, 11–13

Columbines growing on the slopes of Mount Gilboa.

JOY RESTORED

Create a pure heart in me, O God,
and put a new and loyal spirit in me.
Do not banish me from your presence;
do not take your holy spirit away from me.
Give me again the joy that comes from your
salvation,
and make me willing to obey you.
Then I will teach sinners your commands,
and they will turn back to you.

Spare my life, O God, and save me,
and I will gladly proclaim your righteousness.
Help me to speak, Lord,
and I will praise you.

PSALM 51:10–14

A lone donkey-rider takes a road by a stream.

GOD IS A GREAT KING

Clap your hands for joy, all peoples!
Praise God with loud songs!
The Lord, the Most High, is to be feared;
he is a great king, ruling over all the world.
He gave us victory over the peoples;
he made us rule over the nations.
He chose for us the land where we live,
the proud possession of his people,
whom he loves.

God goes up to his throne.
There are shouts of joy and the blast of trumpets,
as the Lord goes up.
Sing praise to God;
sing praise to our king!
God is king over all the world;
praise him with songs!

PSALM 47:1–7

A flight of stone steps at Ephesus, Turkey.

RULER OF ALL THINGS

Come, let us praise the Lord!
Let us sing for joy to God, who protects us!
Let us come before him with thanksgiving
and sing joyful songs of praise.

For the Lord is a mighty God,
a mighty king over all the gods.
He rules over the whole earth,
from the deepest caves to the highest hills.
He rules over the sea, which he made;
the land also, which he himself formed.

Come, let us bow down and worship him;
let us kneel before the Lord, our Maker!
He is our God
we are the people he cares for,
the flock for which he provides.

PSALM 95:1–7

The sun rises over the waters of the Dead Sea, deeper below
sea level than any other lake in the world.

TRUE HAPPINESS

Listen to my words, O Lord,
and hear my sighs.
Listen to my cry for help,
my God and king!

I will pray to you, O Lord;
you hear my voice in the morning;
at sunrise I offer up my prayer
and wait for your answer . . .

Because of your great love
I can come into your house;
I can worship in your holy Temple,
and bow down to you in reverence.
Lord, I have so many enemies!
Lead me to do your will;
make your way plain for me to follow.

All who find safety in you will rejoice;
they can always sing for joy.
Protect those who love you;
because of you they are truly happy.
You bless those who obey you, Lord;
your love protects them like a shield.

PSALM 5:1–3, 7–8, 11–12

The light gleams on the ancient stones of a road nearly 2,000
years old.

THE COURTS OF THE LORD

How I love your Temple, Almighty God!
How I want to be there!
I long to be in the Lord's temple.
With my whole being I sing with joy
to the living God.

Even the sparrows have built a nest,
and the swallows have their own home;
they keep their young near your altars,
Lord Almighty, my king and my God.

How happy are those who live in your Temple,
always singing praise to you!

PSALM 84:1–4

A natural temple is formed by the fronds of palms near the
River Jordan.

VICTORY FEAST

Praise the Lord!

Sing a new song to the Lord;
praise him in the assembly of his faithful people!
Be glad, Israel, because of your Creator;
rejoice, people of Zion, because of your king!
Praise his name with dancing;
play drums and harps in praise of him.

The Lord takes pleasure in his people;
he honors the humble with victory.
Let God's people rejoice in their triumph,
and sing joyfully all night long.

PSALM 149:1–5

A desert-dweller offers hospitality in his tent.

RETURN FROM EXILE

When the Lord brought us back to Jerusalem,
it was like a dream!
How we laughed, how we sang for joy!
Then the other nations said about us,
"The Lord did great things for them!"
Indeed he did great things for us;
how happy we were!

Lord, take us back to our land,
just as the rain brings water back to dry
riverbeds.
Let those who wept as they planted their crops,
gather the harvest with joy!

Those who wept as they went out carrying the
seed
will come back singing for joy,
as they bring in the harvest.

PSALM 126

An old man in the ancient town of Tsefat, Israel.

SADNESS INTO JOY

You have changed my sadness into a joyful
dance;
you have taken away my sorrow
and surrounded me with joy.
So I will not be silent;
I will sing praise to you.
Lord, you are my God.
I will give you thanks forever.

PSALM 30:11–12

Brightly-colored traditional cloths laid out for sale in the
market at Beersheba.

GOD IS NEAR

You, Lord, are all I have,
and you give me all I need;
my future is in your hands.
How wonderful are your gifts to me;
how good they are!

I praise the Lord, because he guides me,
and in the night my conscience warns me.
I am always aware of the Lord's presence;
he is near, and nothing can shake me.

And so I am thankful and glad,
and I feel completely secure;
because you protect me from the power of death
and the one you love you will not abandon to
the world of the dead.

You will show me the path that leads to life;
your presence fills me with joy
and brings me pleasure forever.

PSALM 16:5–11

The sun gleams on a lake in central Turkey while the storm
clouds gather.

JOY IN HARVEST

You show your care for the land by sending rain;
you make it rich and fertile.
You fill the streams with water
You provide the earth with crops.
This is how you do it:

you send abundant rain on the plowed fields
and soak them with water;
you soften the soil with showers
and cause the young plants to grow.

What a rich harvest your goodness provides!
Wherever you go there is plenty.
The pastures are filled with flocks;
the hillsides are full of joy.
The fields are covered with sheep;
the valleys are full of wheat.
Everything shouts and sings for joy.

PSALM 65:9–13

Donkeys pull a sled to thresh the corn in the hills of Judea.

A LIGHT FOR MY PATH

How I love your law!
I think about it all day long.
Your commandment is with me all the time
and makes me wiser than my enemies . . .
How sweet is the taste of your instructions—
sweeter even than honey!
I gain wisdom from your laws,
and so I hate all bad conduct.

Your word is a lamp to guide me
and a light for my path . . .
Your commandments are my eternal possession;
they are the joy of my heart.

PSALM 119:97–98, 103–105, 111

A pale sun gleams over the waters of the Mediterranean.

GOD CARES

I will praise you, Lord, with all my heart;
I will tell of all the wonderful things you have
done.
I will sing with joy because of you.
I will sing praise to you, Almighty God . . .

The Lord is a refuge for the oppressed,
a place of safety in times of trouble.
Those who know you, Lord, will trust you;
you do not abandon anyone who comes to you.

Sing praise to the Lord, who rules in Zion!
Tell every nation what he has done!
God remembers those who suffer;
he does not forget their cry,
and he punishes those who wrong them.

PSALM 9:1–2, 9–12

A woman in the old city of Jerusalem, her load carried on her
head.

LET THE PEOPLE REJOICE

God, be merciful to us and bless us;
look on us with kindness,
so that the whole world may know your will;
so that all nations may know your salvation.

May the peoples praise you, O God;
may all the peoples praise you!

May the nations be glad and sing for joy,
because you judge the peoples with justice
and guide every nation on earth.

May the peoples praise you, O God;
May all the peoples praise you!

The land has produced its harvest;
God, our God, has blessed us.
God has blessed us;
may all people everywhere honor him.

PSALM 67

Two little girls enjoy a game in a narrow street of old
Jerusalem.

THE KING IS GLAD

The king is glad, O Lord, because you gave him
strength;
he rejoices because you made him victorious.
You have given him his heart's desire;
you have answered his request.

You came to him with great blessings
and set a crown of gold on his head.
He asked for life, and you gave it,
a long and lasting life.

His glory is great because of your help;
you have given him fame and majesty.
Your blessings are upon him forever,
and your presence fills him with joy.

PSALM 21:1–6

The remains of the ancient splendors of Avdat, city of the
Negev desert, are silhouetted against the setting sun.

JOY IN OLD AGE

You have taught me ever since I was young,
and I still tell of your wonderful acts.
Now that I am old and my hair is gray,
do not abandon me, O God!
Be with me while I proclaim your power and
might
to all generations to come. . .

I will indeed praise you with the harp;
I will praise your faithfulness, my God.
On my harp I will play hymns to you,
the Holy One of Israel.
I will shout for joy as I play for you;
with my whole being I will sing   .
because you have saved me.

PSALM 71:17–18, 22–23

Old age and youth in a town in central Turkey.

JOYFUL THANKS

How good it is to give thanks to you, O Lord,
to sing in your honor, O Most High God,
to proclaim your constant love every morning
and your faithfulness every night,
with the music of stringed instruments,
and with melody on the harp.
Your mighty deeds, O Lord, make me glad;
because of what you have done, I sing for joy.

PSALM 92:1–4

A reconstruction of a frieze of Assyrian musicians, from the
time of the Psalms (from the Haifa Music Museum).

SING FOR JOY

Sing for joy to the Lord, all the earth;
praise him with songs and shouts of joy!
Sing praises to the Lord!
Play music on the harps!
Blow trumpets and horns,
and shout for joy to the Lord, our king!

Roar, sea, and every creature in you;
sing, earth, and all who live on you!
Clap your hands, you rivers;
you hills, sing together with joy before the Lord,
because he comes to rule the earth.
He will rule the peoples of the world with justice
and fairness.

PSALM 98:4–9

Beyond the breakers the long hump of Mount Carmel juts
out into the sea.